A Concise Account Of

church history

WITH QUESTIONS FOR GROUP STUDY

by
JOHN D. COX

D1498848

Christian Bookstore

GOLDEN RULE SERVICE

749 N.W. Broad Street • Murfreesboro, TN 37129
Phone 615.893.8322 • Fax 615.896.7447 • 1.800.695.5385
Email dehoff@bellsouth.net • www.dehoffbooks.com

Printed in the United States of America

DEDICATION

To my Mother and to the memory of my Father, who brought me up " in the nurture and admonition of the Lord;" to my wife, Myrtle Mae, whose loyalty has been a source of deep encouragement for a score of years through the trials and triumphs of gospel labors; to my daughter, Linda Lane, who is a joy and an inspiration as I "press on toward the goal;" and to my intimate friend, Howard A. White, who has given valuable assistance in arranging the material in this book and in correcting the manuscript.

FOREWORD

In giving a reason for his hope, the well informed Christian must have an accurate knowledge of the Scriptures. He will be even better prepared to support the truth if he also has some understanding of the ways in which men have departed from the Bible through the ages. A study of church history is valuable for this purpose.

The present work has been prepared for the kind of people who heard Jesus most gladly, the common people. The style is therefore admirably simple, and the technical aspects of scholarship have been kept within limits. At the same time, however, the work is based upon sound study and research, and it is believed that all the facts as stated are in harmony with Scriptural and historical truth. This study accordingly contains references to a sufficient variety of sources to enable an interested reader to make further investigations for himself.

The book will be profitable for individual study or for class use. In the latter field it will occupy a unique position and will fill a need long felt by many teachers.

John D. Cox, the author, is one of the most faithful and able preachers among us. Through many years of diligent labor in preaching and teaching he has realized the need for such a work as this and has acquired the technique of stating the truth in a clear and forceful manner. In making the results of his study and experience available to the brotherhood, he has rendered a distinct service.

Howard A. White

CONTENTS

Chapter I

THE NEW TESTAMENT CHURCH

The purpose of these lessons: To trace the facts of history with reference to the church: its establishment; its doctrine and practice in the beginning; the steps which culminated in a great falling away from the truth; the many attempts to return to the New Testament pattern, and the success of many of these efforts.

A study of this kind should prove profitable for a number of reasons. It should help us to have a greater appreciation for the church as it was in the beginning. It should serve as a warning against the introduction of innovations and errors, slight departures from God's plan, no matter how innocent and insignificant they may appear. It should afford honest seekers after the truth an opportunity to know how and why the various denominations came into existence. The author pledges himself to an honest effort to present only such historical facts as may be verified by authentic sources. He shall earnestly endeavor to deal with the facts of history in the light of the word of God without prejudice.

Jesus promised to build his church. He said to Peter, "Upon this rock I will build my church, and the gates of Hades shall not prevail against it."[1] Since Christ was the builder of his church, it was built by a

---

1 *Matt.* 16.18.

7

divine pattern. A house built by any other is not recognized by the Lord. "Except Jehovah build the house, they labor in vain that build it."[2] Jesus said: "Every plant which my heavenly Father planted not shall be rooted up."[3] The church of the New Testament is exactly as the Lord would have it. God never intended that man should alter the divinely given pattern in any way. All changes from this divine pattern that have marked the history of man's religious activities have been without the authority of the word of God. Let us consider the distinctive features of the church that Jesus built.

I. MARKS OF THE NEW TESTAMENT CHURCH

1. Christ is the builder or founder of the New Testament Church. He promised to build but one church, and we have a record of only one being established by his authority. Therefore, this is truly a distinctive feature of the New Testament church. The only church upon the earth that can truthfully claim Christ as its founder is the church that we read about in the New Testament.

2. Christ is the foundation of the New Testament church. After Peter had confessed his faith in Christ as the Son of God, Jesus said, "Upon this rock," that is, the bed-rock foundation fact that he was the Son of God, "I will build my church." That he was speaking of himself and not Peter as the foundation of the church is clearly seen from what the Holy Spirit said through Paul, "For other foundation can no man lay than that which is laid, which is Jesus Christ."[4] This

---

2 *Ps.* 127:1.
3 *Matt.* 15:13.

4 *1 Cor.* 3:11.

leaves no room for argument as to the foundation of the New Testament church. Paul tells us that the foundation was already laid; that it was Christ; and that no man can lay another foundation.

3. Another distinctive feature of the church of the New Testament is that it has no source of authority save Christ and his word. "For I am not ashamed of the gospel of Christ: for it is the power of God unto salvation to everyone that believeth; to the Jew first, and also to the Greek."[5] "Every scripture inspired of God is also profitable for teaching, for reproof, for correction, for instruction which is in righteousness: that the man of God may be complete, furnished completely unto every good work."[6] To become and be a member of the New Testament church the word of God is the only creed or book of religion that is needed. It is authoritative; it is simple; it is complete; it is unchanging.

4. The names by which the members of the New Testament church are to be known have been designated by God in the divine pattern. Religious names given by men are wrong. They are wrong, first of all, because there is no scriptural authority for them. They are wrong, in the second place, because they foster strife and division among the professed followers of Christ. The Holy Spirit rebuked the church at Corinth because of divisions that were occasioned by the members attaching themselves to men and wearing their names. Paul wrote to the church at Corinth, "For it hath been signified unto me concerning you, my brethren, by them that are of the household of Chloe, that there are contentions among you. Now

---

5 *Rom.* 1:16.   6 *2 Tim.* 3:16, 17.

this I mean, that each one of you saith, I am of Paul;
and I of Apollos; and I of Cephas; and I of Christ. Is
Christ divided? was Paul crucified for you? or were
ye baptized into the name of Paul? I thank God that I
baptized none of you, save Crispus and Gaius; lest any
man should say that ye were baptized into my name."[7]
These words of inspiration emphasize the truth that
human names in religion have no place in the divine
pattern.   In the third chapter of this same epistle,
their divisions and the wearing of human names is
pointed out as evidence of their carnality.[8]   In the
New Testament, individual members of the church
are called "Christians."[9] Collectively, or as a church,
they are called by various names, such as, "the church
of God."[10] "The churches of Christ,"[11] "the church
of the Lord,"[12] "the church,"[13] "the 'body' of Christ,"
[14] the "church of the firstborn,"[15] and "the kingdom
of the Son of his love."[16]   By a careful study of the
New Testament pattern of the church, the thoughtful
reader will be impressed with the absence of the popular denominational names which are heard on every
hand today.   It is strange, indeed, that so many unscriptural names are worn today by those who claim to
follow Christ, when Bible names are sufficient and
would serve as a basis of unity in religion.

5. Contrary to the practice of the Jews under the
law of Moses, the New Testament church met for worship upon the first day of the week.[17] The worship
in which the members of the church engaged was sim-

7 *1 Cor.* 1:11-15.
8 *1 Cor.* 3:3.
9 *Acts.* 11:26; *1 Pet.* 4:16
10 *1 Cor.* 1:2.
11 *Rom.* 16:16.
12 *Acts* 20:28.
13 *Acts* 2:47.
14 *Eph.* 1:22.
15 *Heb.* 12:23.
16 *Col.* 1:13.
17 *Acts.* 20:7.

ple and spiritual. Jesus directed that his followers worship God "in spirit and truth." [18] Three outstanding points characterized the worship: 1. It was directed toward the right object: God. 2. It was prompted by the right attitude of heart: in spirit. 3. It involved the right action: according to truth.

6. The truth reveals that the New Testament church engaged in the following items of worship: 1. The word of God was taught,[19] 2. The Lord's Supper was eaten in memory of Christ.[20] As they ate the bread and drank the fruit of the vine, they remembered the death of Christ and looked forward to his return. The worship actually centered around this feast which was a communion of the body and blood of the Lord. Today, many who attempt to worship God while engaging in other items that are found in the New Testament, omit the one to which the early disciples seemed to attach the greatest importance upon the first day of the week. 3. Congregational prayer was engaged in as an item of worship.[21] 4 They gave of their means upon the first day of the week as the Lord had prospered them. [22] This giving was done cheerfully, regularly, and with purpose of heart. The practice of selling merchandise or presenting programs of entertainment to raise money was unknown to the New Testament church. 5. They praised God in song, making melody with the heart. [23] The music of the church consisted only of singing. Mechanical instruments of music are not to be found in the New Testament pattern of worship. There were to be found no lords in high places, but the members of the church were ser-

---

18 *Jno.* 4:24.
19 *Acts.* 2:42.
20 *1 Cor.* 11:26; *Acts* 20:7
21 *Acts* 2:42.
22 *1 Cor.* 16:2.
23 *Col.* 3:16; *Eph.* 5:19.

vants. There was no distinction such as is known to-day as the "clergy" and the "laity".

The local churches were independent, each congregation being a unit within itself. All congregations were equally related to Christ. They were not bound together under earthly ecclesiastical or denominational authority in conferences, conventions, synods or the like. The organization of the church consisted simply of elders and deacons in each congregation. [24]

There were no missionary societies, but preaching the gospel at home and abroad was done as a work of the church.

8. The terms of membership in the church were clearly set forth. They were identical with the instructions of Christ in the Great Commission. [25] In this commission Jesus taught that faith, repentance, and baptism are pre-requisites to the remission of sins. It was this that the New Testament church preached and practiced. It was understood by the members that the doctrine of Christ was essential to salvation. [26] It was not only understood that the gospel of Christ was essential, but also that is was the only doctrine authorized by God. Where the doctrine of God is referred to in the New Testament, it is in the singular. False doctrines were spoken of as though there were many, but the doctrine of God was set forth as being one.

9. The unity of organization and practice which necessarily followed unity of doctrine was a distinctive feature of the New Testament church. Christ had prayed that his followers should all be one. [27] And we read of the "one body", which was placed in com-

24 *Acts* 14:23; 20:17; Phil. 1:1.
25 *Matt.* 28:18-20; *Mk.* 16:- 15, 16; *Lk.* 24:45, 46.
26 *Rom.* 1:16.
27 *Jno.* 17:20, 21.

pany with a group of "ones" in the plan of salvation: one body, one Spirit, one hope, one Lord, one faith, one baptism, and one God. [28] And this one body is described as being the church over which Christ is the head. [29]

II. THE CHURCH AT THE CLOSE OF THE NEW TESTAMENT PERIOD

At the close of the New Testament period, the church was characterized by unity of doctrine, worship, name, organization, and work. Warnings had been issued by the apostles that a departure from the divine pattern would come, as the following statements of scripture will show. Paul said to the elders of the church at Ephesus: "I know that after my departing, grievous wolves shall enter in among you, not sparing the flock; and from among your own selves shall men arise, speaking perverse things, to draw away the disciples after them."[30] "But the Spirit saith expressly, that in later times some shall fall away from the faith, giving heed to seducing spirits and doctrines of demons, through the hypocrisy of men that speak lies, branded in their own conscience as with a hot iron; forbidding to marry, and commanding to abstain from meats."[31] "For the time will come when they will not endure sound doctrine; but, having itching ears, will heap to themselves teachers after their own lusts; and will turn away their ears from the truth, and turn aside unto fables."[32]

It happened as these New Testament writers predicted. To trace the steps through which this great

---

28 *Eph.* 4:4-6.
29 *Eph.* 1:22.
30 *Acts.* 20:28-30.
31 1 *Tim.* 4: 1-3.
32 2 *Tim.* 4:2-4.

apostasy came about is the purpose of this series of studies.

CONCLUSION

The summary above gives us a picture of the church as God established it. A study of this divine pattern for the church will cause one to be filled with bewilderment as he realizes how far men have departed from this pattern in their religious activities. The question is often asked by honest persons: "Where did so many denominations come from?" Many have asked this question and then being ignorant of the facts of history, have sought the answer by assuming that since denominationalism exists it must be right. To take this attitude is merely to "hide one's head in the sand." All know that the existence of a thing or state of affairs does not necessarily justify it. If is wrong, it is wrong no matter how well established it may be. Just so, a look at the New Testament pattern, in which is set forth a state of unity among the followers of Christ, proves without doubt that the divisions and multiplicity of doctrines which are propagated by hundreds of denominations are wrong. "Where did so many denominations come from?" The author promises to answer this question with established historical facts in the course of this study.

QUESTIONS

1. State the purpose of this course of study in your own words.

2. Why should a study of this kind prove profitable?

3. How do we know that the church was built by a divine pattern?

4. Where may we expect to find this pattern revealed?

5. What change does God permit man to make in the pattern of his church?

6. How many churches did Jesus build?

7. How many foundations has the New Testament church had? Give Scripture.

8. What doctrine, authorized by God, was subscribed to by the early Christians?

9. By what name were individual members of the New Testament church known?

10. Give some of the names by which they were called collectively.

11. Point out the evils involved in wearing man-made names in religion.

12. Give Paul's argument to the church at Corinth as to why they should serve God in the name of Christ only.

13. Discuss the difference in the day of worship under the Jewish and Christian dispensations. List all the Scriptures you can find on this subject.

14. What items of worship were engaged in by members of the New Testament church?

15. How have many departed from this pattern?

16. Explain, in your own words, the organization of the church as authorized by God.

17. From observing the organization of the various denominations, what departures from God's plan have you noticed?

18. What were the terms of membership in the New Testament church?

19. What are some of the changes in this respect that have been introduced by the various religious groups?

20. Explain the difference in the unity that characterized the New Testament church and the modern "federation" of churches which many regard as the unity of organization that pleases God?

21. What warning was issued by the apostles before the close of the New Testament period?

Chapter II

THE CHURCH DURING THE
ANTE-NICENE PERIOD

Attention has been called to the divine pattern for the church as it is revealed on the pages of the New Testament. The church as we see it in the New Testament was just as God wanted it. It was characterized by unity of doctrine, organization, worship and work. Various New Testament writers sounded a note of warning that a great apostasy would take place——men would depart from the faith, speaking perverse things.

We now turn to secular history and begin the arduous task of tracing the development of various circumstances and ideas which presented themselves after the close of the New Testament period. The particular period of church history in which we are interested in this lesson is what is known as "The Ante-Nicene Period." By "Ante-Nicene period" is meant the period between the close of the New Testament and the Council of Nicea (325 A.D.) at which the Nicene Creed was adopted.

I. THE CONDITION OF THE ROMAN WORLD

At the time that Christianity had its beginning, the Roman Empire was ruled by men placed at its head by the army. The population consisted of three class-

17

es: the wealthy, the slaves, and the middle class of free-citizens. The wealthy lolled in luxury, being served by their slaves.

> The poorer classes only lived for bread and circuses. The circuses were brutal, debasing, and bloody; . . . The nation groaned under heavy taxation that went for such a waste and extravagance . . . The state came first, the home had little place in Paganism. Women were considered as chattel property; and little children were often cruelly mistreatd; and if born deformed, or their parents did not want them, they were exposed to die, or killed. 1

Most of the emperors were cruel, wicked and extravagant. "It was into such a morally degenerate, sensual, and cruel world that Christianity was thrust, to conquer and raise to a fit place in which to live."2

PERSECUTIONS AGAINST THE EARLY CHURCH

During the New Testament period of the church its members were subjected to various attacks by the enemies of Christianity. At the first, the source of persecution was the Jews. But, when the Roman government began to recognize Christianity as a religion separate from Judaism, it was regarded as an illegal religion. Christians then came under the fire of heathen persecutors.

In the life-time of the apostles, the two main waves of persecution which swept over the church at the hands of heathen rulers were waged by Nero (A.D. 65-68) and Domitian (A.D. 89-96).

Of the persecution by Nero, Fisher says,

> The first marked instance of heathen enmity on record was the persecution under Nero. It is described by the Roman historian Tacitus. From his account we see that the

1 Homer Hailey, "The Church In The Ante-Nicene Period," *Abilene Christian College Lectures* (Abilene, Texas, 1934), 18,
2 *Ibid.* I, 19.

Christians were then well known as a distinct sect. Nero, who was justly detested for his brutal tyranny, in order to avert from himself what was, perhaps, a groundless suspicion of having set Rome on fire, accused the Christians of having kindled the flames which had laid in ashes a great part of the city. [3] Fisher quotes from Tacitus who tells how a "vast multitude were convicted . . . And in their deaths they were made the subjects of sport, for they were covered with hides of wild beasts, and worried to death by dogs, or nailed to crosses, or set fire to, and when day declined were burned to serve for nocturnal lights."[4]

The persecution of the emperor Domitian reached its height about A.D. 95. Domitian is described by historians as a cruel and worthless ruler with a jealous temper. He caused hundreds of believers to be put to death. Among those who perished was his own cousin. Many were banished and the property of others was confiscated.

SOME PRINCIPAL PERSECUTORS AND SOME PROMINENT MARTYRS AFTER THE CLOSE OF THE NEW TESTAMENT PERIOD

It will be impossible to mention and discuss all heathen rulers who had a part in persecuting the followers of Christ during this period. Reference will be made to some of the principal ones.

About 111 A.D., Pliny, governor of Bithynia, wrote letters to the emperor Trajan calling his attention to a problem that had been created in his district by the increasing number of Christians. He called Christianity a "superstition" and expressed concern because so many had become Christians that the temples of the heathen gods were almost forsaken.

---

3 George P. Fisher, *History of the Christian Church* (New York, 1945), 31.
    4 *Ibid.*

Those who made their living by selling animals to be sacrificed to heathen gods had suffered great loss in business. Pliny desired instruction as to how to treat these Christians. Trajan replied that they were to be left alone unless they were prosecuted by accusers who would give their names. If convicted, they were to be given an opportunity to renounce their faith in Christ. If they refused, they were to be punished. While this appeared to be lenient in a way, at the same time it laid the way open for wholesale persecutions by unscrupulous men who were willing to accuse and testify against the Christians falsely.

One of the most prominent martyrs under the reign of Trajan was Ignatius of Antioch. While being taken to Rome he exhorted Christians on the way and prayed that he might have the honor of dying for Christ. He was thrown to the wild beasts in the Roman amphitheatre about 108 A.D. Fox's Book of Martyrs says that as Ignatius heard the roaring of the lions, he shouted: "I am the wheat of Christ: I am going to be ground with the teeth of wild beasts, that I may be found pure bread."[5]

Marcius Aurelius, who reigned from 161 to 180 A. D., is described as a just and virtuous ruler, and yet he poured out bitter persecutions upon the followers of Christ. He was determined to restore the ancient religious practices and the old Roman way of life. He regarded the Christians as innovators and, therefore, sought to suppress them by force. He used many cruel means in putting believers to death. A prominent martyr during his reign was Polycarp. He

5 Fox's Book of Martyrs, William B. Forbush, ed. (Philadelphia, 1926), 8.

was brought before the governor and called upon to curse the name of Jesus Christ. His reply was: "Six and eighty years have I served him, and he has done me nothing but good; and how could I curse him, my Lord and Savior!"[6] Whereupon, he was burned to death. (155 A. D.)

The followers of Christ were persecuted by emperor after emperor through the years, some fierce, others mild. A period of peace from persecutions was introduced by the reign of Gallineus in 260 A.D. which lasted for about forty years. During this period, large expensive church buildings were erected and the church became rich, its members worldly and contentious.

The most formidable and systematic of all the persecutions of this period was the last one which was waged by Diocletian in 303. He was a man of great talents as a statesman and was a conservative Roman. He "determined to exterminate Christianity and to reinstate the ancient system of worship."[7] Hurlbut describes the drastic measures of Diocletian in the following statement:

In a series of edicts it was ordered that every copy of the Bible should be burned; that all churches—which had arisen throughout the empire during the half-century of comparative rest from persecutions—should be torn down; that all who would not renounce the Christian religion should lose their citizenship and be outside the protection of the law. In some places the Christians were assembled in their churches, which were set on fire and burned with all the worshipers within their walls.[8]

Rest came to the church from persecution by

6 Fisher, *History of the Christian Church* 48.
7 *Ibid.* 50.
8 Jesse Lyman Hurlbut *The Story of the Christian Church* (Philadelphia 1933) 56.

heathen emperors in 313 A.D. when Constantine issued his Edict of Toleration. "By this law Christianity
was sanctioned, its worship was made lawful, and all
persecution ceased, not to be renewed while the Roman
Empire endured." [9]

IV. REASONS FOR THESE PERSECUTIONS.

Upon first thought it might be regarded as strange
that a body of religious believers so harmless as the
followers of Christ should be the object of such bitter
wrath as that which was poured out by these heathen
rulers. But a reflection upon certain facts and circumstances will help one to see why this occurred.

1. Heathenism welcomed many gods. The Romans
were noted for their multiplicity of gods. Christianity,
however, opposed all worship except to the one God,
Jehovah.

2. Idol worship was interwoven with all phases of
life among the Roman citizens. Christians refused to
offer sacrifices to these false gods. Consequently, they
were branded as atheists and enemies of their fellow-
men.

3. Emperor worship was required of all. Christians
refused to "bow down" before the emperor's image.
For this reason they failed to pass the chief test of
loyalty to the State.

4. After the destruction of Jerusalem, Christianity
came to be regarded as an offspring of Jewish fanati-
cism.

5. The secret meetings of the Christians, as they
assembled in the caves and catacombs for worship,

9 *Ibid.* 57.

aroused suspicion. Wild rumors spread abroad as to the real purpose of these meetings.

6. Christianity looked upon all as equals. It made no distinction between master and slaves. This, of course, was contrary to the spirit of the Roman world.

7. Business interests often caused Christians to be persecuted. When those who made and sold images saw their business hindered because multitudes were turning from idol gods to serve the living God, they sought to suppress Christianity.

8. Another cause of persecution against believers was superstition. They were charged with causing famines, pestilences, and plagues in the land.

9. The influence of pagan philosophies which were propagated by the Stoics and Epicureans caused men to look down upon Christianity because it was accepted by the common and unlettered class, and because it preached a system of faith and did not prove anything on philosophical grounds. Modernists object to Christianity on the same ground today——that it is a system of blind faith. Those who reject Christ as the Son of God may profess great learning and depth of thought as they talk glibly of the blindness of Christianity. But, it should be remembered that this idea is not a new discovery with them; they borrowed it from pagan philosophers!

V. BEHAVIOR OF CHRISTIANS UNDER PERSECUTION

Under the terrors of persecution, there were many who lacked the courage to endure and so renounced their faith in Christ to save their lives. Thousands, however, held their faith as dearer than their lives and all earthly things. These suffered untold agony, and many died rather than to deny Christ who died for them. The meekness and undaunted faith and courage of those Christians under persecution became more than a match for all the armed power of Rome. Their example is an inspiration to Christians in all ages to stand firm in the faith. Persecutions of today may be in different forms from those suffered by early Christians, but regardless of whether it comes in the form of bodily harm, ridicule, or slander we must endure. Christ suffered for us; why should we not be willing to suffer for him?

QUESTIONS

1. What is meant by "Ante-Nicene Period?"

2. In your own words, tell of conditions in the Roman Empire at the time Christianity was first planted upon the earth.

3. What people first persecuted Christianity?

4. Why did the Roman government begin to persecute Christians?

5. Tell of the two main waves of persecution against the church in the days of the apostles.

6. What problem confronted Pliny, governor of Bithynia?

7. What was the result of Trajan's reply to Pliny's letter?

8. When and how did Ignatius of Antioch meet his death?

9. During whose reign was Polycarp burned to death?

10. What statement, now famous, was made by Polycarp just before his death?

11. What valuable contribution did Justin Martyr make to religious literature?

12. What is to be remembered about the reign of Gallineus, 260 A.D.?

13. Tell what you know of Diocletian and the persecution waged by him against Christianity.

14. What was the "Edict of Toleration?"

15. State, briefly, the reasons for these persecutions against Christians.

16. Can any of these be applied to Christians under present-day conditions?

17. Describe the behavior of the Christians under persecution.

18. What lesson is there in this for us?

CHAPTER III

THE CHURCH DURING THE
ANTE-NICENE PERIOD
(Concluded)

In the preceding chapter the various stages of imperial persecutions against the church were discussed. It was during this same period that the organization of the church began to undergo a gradual change which marked the beginning of a great apostasy.

The apostles had definitely foretold that a falling away would take place. They had even warned that false teachers would arise from within the church, even from among its elders, speaking perverse things to draw away the disciples after them. [1] In view of the predictions of the apostles, it is interesting to notice that the first departure from the New Testament pattern which history records did take place through the action of some elders of the church of the Lord.

I. CHANGES IN ORGANIZATION

Sometime during the second century the practice was introduced of selecting one of the elders to preside over the meetings as a permanent president. This elder was called the "bishop" to distinguish him from the other elders. The New Testament applies the terms "elders" and "bishops" to the same men in the church. No distinction was made among them in rank

---

1 *Acts* 20:28-31; *2 Tim.* 4:1-6; 2:1-12.

or authority. When this distinction in name was introduced, of course it was followed by a distinction of authority. The bishop came to be recognized as having greater voice in the affairs of the church than the other elders. The authority of the bishop increased until each bishop was assigned a definite territory over which to rule or have the oversight. This territory was called a diocese. In some cases the diocese was so large that one bishop could not look after it, and this situation called for a division of the territory. In this way, another class of officer was created. He was called the "Chorepiscopus" or "Country Bishop." His rank was midway between the "City Bishop" and the elders.

Various questions and problems would arise and it was thought necessary for the Bishop and Presbyters or elders to meet and discuss them. This gave rise to the practice of calling occasional conventions. This idea grew until these conventions took on the nature of permanent institutions and were known as Synods and Councils. They were called *synods* by the Greeks and *councils* by the Latins. Those who attended these meetings gradually became legislative bodies with power to decide issues and make decrees for the churches.

The Councils and Synods were presided over by the bishops of the churches from the chief cities. This naturally augmented the power of these Bishops. The position of president of a council soon came to be regarded as an office within itself. The situation called for a name to distinguish this officer from other bishops in the church. So a new name in church organization was added to the already growing list of unscriptual offices and officers. Those who presided over the councils were called *metropolitans*.

Up to the fourth century these Councils or Synods were held in the various provinces over which the Metropolitans ruled and each Metropolitan was independent of all the other Metropolitans in the government of his province. (In) 325 A. D. the emperor Constantine called the first General Ecumenical Council. This Council was composed of Commissioners from all the churches of the Christian World and represented the Church Universal. 2

The ecclesiastical rulers who were placed over these larger districts were called patriarchs, which means "chief fathers." At first there were only three patriarchs; at Rome, Alexandria and Antioch. Later, the bishops of Jerusalem and Constantinople were made Patriarchs, making five in all.

A study of these facts of history should serve as a solemn reminder that small beginnings in the wrong direction may result in wide departures from the truth of God. The organization of the church underwent so many changes that it held no resemblance to the New Testament pattern. God's way was for each congregation to have elders and deacons. The elders were also called bishops, pastors and presbyters.

As the movement began away from this simple plan, first we see one elder distinguished from others as the bishop; then there were city bishops and country bishops; next there came the metropolitans; then the patriarchs. This brings us to within one step of the pope who gained power over both church and state.

2 George A. Klingman *Church History For Busy People* (Cincinnati, 1928) 13.

Of this change in the organization of the church, Mosheim says,

Hence, it came to pass that, at the conclusion of this century (4th Century), there remained no more than a mere shadow of the ancient government of the church. Many of the privileges which had formerly belonged to the presbyters and people were usurped by the bishops, and many of the rights, which had been formerly vested in the universal church, were transferred to the emperors, and to subordinate officers and magistrates. [3]

II. DISTINCTION BETWEEN CLERGY AND LAITY

Another departure from the New Testament pattern which gradually took place along with the changes of church organization was the distinction between preachers and other members of the church. By the close of the Second Century the idea began to take shape that the ministry possessed the attributes of the priesthood. This idea borrowed support from Judaism. The effect was that the clergy came to be exalted in the popular opinion as a higher order and was separated from the laity. This idea has manifested itself in various ways and to varying degrees in the different religious groups down through the years. It is because of this that preachers and religious leaders have dared to wear such titles as *father* and *reverend* which belong only to God.

When we consider the arrogance and the utter lack of humility which characterizes many who stand in the pulpits of our land today, we cannot help but recall the unassuming nature and the deep humility which filled the lives of such men of God as Peter and

---

3 John L. Mosheim, *An Eccesiastical History, Ancient And Modern From The Birth Of Christ To The Beginning Of The Present Century,* 6 Vols., Archibald McClain, ed. (Philadelphia, 1797), 339.

Paul. When Peter arrived at Caesarea and was met by Cornelius, who fell at his feet and worshipped him, he raised him up saying, "Stand up, I myself also am a man."[4]

When the multitudes of Lystra made ready their sacrifices that they might offer them in worship to Paul and Barnabas as gods, these gospel preachers rent their garments and sprang forth among the multitudes, crying out and saying, "Sirs, why do ye these things? We also are men of like passions with you, and bring you good tidings, that ye should turn from these vain things unto a living God."[5]

The apostles and other New Testament preachers being our example, there is nothing at all in the divine record to justify the practice of having preachers to dress differently from other members of the church and of giving them glorious titles which the Bible ascribes to God.

III. THE COUNCIL OF NICEA

Since this lesson brings us to the close of a distinct period in church history known as the Ante-Nicene Period, it is well to close with mention of the Council of Nicea.

In 313 A. D. Constantine issued his Edict of Toleration which officially put an end to the persecutions against Christianity by a pagan government. Christianity had won the victory over heathenism, but no sooner than rest came from persecution by heathen hands, a new conflict arose. There arose a series of controversies within the church over doctrine. The

4 *Acts* 10:24-26.
5 *Acts* 14:13-15.

three outstanding controversies of doctrine which marked this period are known to history as : 1. The Arian Controversy, which had to do with the doctrine of the Trinity, especially the relation of the Father and the Son; 2. The Appolinarian Controversy, with reference to the nature of Christ; 3. The Pelagian Controversy over questions relating to sin and salvation. As has been pointed out, the method of attempting to settle such controversies was to call the church together in councils. At these councils the votes were cast by bishops. Their decisions were bound upon the lower clergy and the laity.

In an effort to calm the trouble which had resulted from the Arian Controversy, Constantine called a council of the bishops which met in Nicea in Bithynia, 325 A.D. It was attended by 318 bishops and was presided over by the emperor Constantine. Creeds were introduced as a basis of compromise. But the final result was the adoption of a formal statement of faith now known as "The Nicene Creed." "The Council adjourned about the middle of August. 'The Creed of Creeds' had been born; Christianity had become the state religion; . . . and civil and ecclesiastical governments were joining hands."[6]

QUESTIONS

1. To Teacher: Lead class in brief review of Chapters I and II.

2. What was the nature of the first departure from the New Testament pattern?

---

6 Hailey, *Abilene Christian College Lectures,* 30.

3. What plan was adopted for settling the various questions and problems which arose?

4. What were these conventions called?

5. Who presided in these meetings?

6. What were these presiding officers called?

7. What is meant by an ecumenical council?

8. When and by whom was the first one called?

9. What was a patriarch?

10. How many were there, and in what cities did they reside?

11. What warning should we take from a study of these matters?

12. In your own words, tell of Mosheim's description of church organization at the close of the Fourth Century.

13. What erroneous notion found a place in the thinking of the people with reference to preachers?

14. Discuss the results of this idea.

15. Compare the attitude of many modern preachers to that of Peter and Paul.

16. What edict did Constantine issue in 313 A.D.? Explain the purpose of it.

17. Name and describe the three outstanding doctrinal controversies of the Ante-Nicene Period.

18. When, by whom, and why was the Council of Nicea called?

19. Where did it convene?

20. What was the result of this council?

Chapter IV.

THE CHURCH DURING THE DARK AGES

In our study thus far, we have considered the New Testament church as it was planted upon the earth according to a divinely given pattern. We have seen that church gradually led into a great apostasy. Men completely changed the organization of the church from the New Testament pattern. Heretical doctrines were introduced, followed by sharp controversy. To settle one of these doctrinal controversies the Roman emperor, Constantine, who was sympathetic toward the church, called the universal church council which met at Nicea in Bithynia 325 A.D. At this council the first human creed (the Nicene Creed) was adopted. Christianity came to be recognizd as the state religion and it was evident that the governments of the church and state were joining hands.

I. THE UNION OF CHURCH AND STATE

This tendency toward the union of the church and civil government suggests a new question to the mind cf the thoughtful student of history, "What is the teaching of Christ and his apostles on the relation of the church to the state?" When asked, "Is it lawful to give tribute to Caesar, or not?" Jesus replied, "Render therefore unto Caesar the things that are Caesar's and unto God the things that are God's."[1] Jesus recognized

---

1 *Matt.* 22:21.

the authority of civil government in secular affairs and taught his followers to live in submission to the laws of the land so long as such laws do not oppose the laws of God. When Jesus said, "Render unto Caesar the things that are Caesar's and unto God the things that are God's," he did more than to place upon his followers the responsibility of seeking to live in submission to both civil and divine laws. He clearly set forth the principle of the separation of the church and the state.

The apostles of Christ commanded Christians to obey existing civil governments as may be seen from the following statements of scripture. "Let every soul be subject to the higher powers: for there is no power but of God; and the powers that be are ordained of God."[2]

"I exhort, therefore, first of all, that supplications, prayers, intercessions, thanksgivings, be made for all men; for kings and all that are in high places; that we may lead a tranquil and quiet life in all godliness and gravity."[3] "Put them in mind to be in subjection to rulers, to authorities, to be obedient, to be ready unto every good work."[4] "Be subject to every ordinance of man for the Lord's sake: Whether to the king, as supreme; or unto governors, as sent by him for vengeance on evil-doers and for praise to them that do well."[5] From these statements we know that it is impossible for one to be a faithful Christian without being a law-abiding citizen. However, while teaching Christians to recognize the authority of civil government, the apostles also charged Christians to put God's au-

2 *Rom.* 13:1.
3 *1 Tim.* 2:1,2.
4 *Tit.* 3:1.
5 *1 Pet.* 2:13,14.

thority above that of civil officers. When officers of the civil law charged the apostles that they should no longer preach the name of Jesus, they replied, "We must obey God rather than men."[6] This accords with the commandment of Christ when he said: "Seek ye first the kingdom of God, and his righteousness; and all these things shall be added unto you."[7] The historical events which will be presented in the course of this series of studies prove that both the church and state can serve the respective purposes which God intended for them only by remaining separate, each seeking to avoid interference with the other.

II. CONSTANTINE—THE FIRST "CHRISTIAN EMPEROR"

In the early part of the fourth century an event occurred which proved to be of momentous importance in the history of the Christian religion. It was nothing less than the "conversion" of a Roman emperor to the Christian religion. While most historians seem to think that Constantine was sincere in his professed belief in the true and living God, all admit that his interest in Christianity was more political than otherwise.

Be that as it may, the fact that a Roman emperor recognized the Christian religion even to the extent of accepting it as his personal religion led the church into an alliance with the state which was to bear consequences both good and evil. The Roman empire, from being the enemy and persecutor of the church, thenceforward became its protector and patron.

In relating his conversion, Constantine claimed that he saw a vision of a flaming cross in the sky

6 *Acts* 5:29.   7 *Matt.* 6:33.

bearing the inscription, "By This Conquer." Fisher suggests that "perhaps" this was an optical illusion caused by an excited imagination.[8] We would drop the word "perhaps." He adopted the standard of the cross which was afterwards carried in his armies. He deferred baptism until the day before his death. Historians are generally agreed that this was due to the fact that he shared in the current belief that baptism was for the remission of sins. His idea of postponing baptism was, of course, erroneous but his conviction as to the purpose of baptism is significant. It is worthy of notice that so soon after the close of the New Testament period the prevalent conception as to the purpose of baptism was that it was essential to salvation from sin. Those who contend that baptism is not essential to salvation not only reject the teaching of the New Testament, but they place themselves against the facts of history which show that as late as the Fourth Century the majority of believers regarded baptism as essential.

III. THE EFFECT OF CONSTANTINE'S REIGN

It goes without saying that such an unusual and unexpected event as the conversion of the emperor to the Christian religion produced many and far reaching results to both the church and the state, some good and some evil.

Among the good results to the church, mention should be made of the following: 1. Imperial persecutions ceased. This was brought about by Constantine's Edict of Toleration in 313 A.D. 2. Church buildings

8 Fisher, *History Of The Christian Church,* 88.

were restored and reopened. 3. Heathenism was discouraged.

Some of the good results to the state which came as a consequence of Constantine's conversion were: 1. The abolishment of crucifixion as a form of execution for criminals. 2. The repression of infanticide. 3. The modification of slavery. The influence of Christianity caused the treatment of slaves to be more humane; and legal rights were given to them which they never possessed before. 4. The contests of gladiators were suppressed.

While the triumph of Christianity resulted in much that was good, many evils also resulted. Hurlbut states:

> The ceasing of persecution was a blessing, but the establishment of Christianity as the State religion became a curse. Everybody sought membership in the church, and nearly everybody was received. Both good and bad, sincere seekers after God and hypocritical seekers after gain, rushed into the communion. Ambitious, worldly, unscrupulous men sought office in the church for social and political influence. [9]

Many passed from heathenism to Christianity by no other conversion than a mere change of name. Pagan forms and ceremonies gradually crept into the worship. Images of saints and martyrs began to appear in the churches. At first, these images were installed as memorials, but later they came to be worshiped. The meaning of the Lord's Supper was changed, in the minds of the worshipers, from a memorial to a sacrifice. It came to be considered as a means of protection and salvation from all dangers and evils and as of great benefit for the souls of the departed. "The adoration of the Virgin Mary was substituted for the worship of Venus and Diana . . . As a result of the

[9] Hurlbut, *The Story Of The Christian Church*, 79.

church sitting in power, we do not see Christianity transforming the world to its own ideal, but the world dominating the church." [10] This was the result of the use of the wrong means in an effort to influence the world. God never intended that the church should be a political machine, but rather a teaching institution. The power of the church to influence both the individuals and the governments of the world for good lies not in political maneuvers, but in the great work of imparting the principles of Christianity by teaching the word of God to all the nations on earth.

IV. THE RISE OF MONASTICISM

As the church became more worldly in its attitudes and actions, there were deeply spiritual souls among the members who rebelled against such a state of affairs. Their disgust gave rise to another movement which culminated in what is now known as monasticism. Anthony of Thebes, who lived about 320 A.D., is considered the founder of monasticism. He retired to a cave where he lived in pious contemplation, struggling to overcome all the evils of his nature. Others who were disgusted with the worldliness in the church followed the practice of Anthony and went to the extreme of withdrawing from the world. The number increased until gradually separated communities grew up and those who dwelled within them were called monks. Similar communities were established for women who sought to withdraw from the world and they were called nuns. All Bible students know that there are no monks or nuns in the New Testament. The spirit of Christianity is just the opposite to the

10 *Ibid.*

spirit of monasticism. Christians are taught to remain
in touch with the world but to conduct themselves in
such a manner as to influence it for good. They are
to be the salt of the earth and the light of the world. [11]
By living the principles of Christianity as we dwell
among men, we may avoid the two extremes of withdrawing from the world on the one hand and of be-
coming as worldly as the world on the other.

V. THE DEVELOPMENT OF PAPAL POWER

In a former lesson attention was called to changes
in the organization of the church which were leading
to the development of an ecclesiastical heirarchy. Let
us return to this phase of our study to notice the development of papal power.

When Rome lost her place as capital of the world
by the founding of Constantinople as the capital of
the Roman Empire in 325 A.D., she began to assert her
right to be the capital of the church.

The five presiding bishops who lived in Jerusalem,
Antioch, Alexandria, Constantinople and Rome were
called "Patriarchs." The Patriarch at Rome took the
title of "papa, father," afterward modified into "pope."
A bitter battle for power was waged among the patriarchs. This battle finally narrowed down to a con-
test between the pope of Rome and the patriarch of
Constantinople as to which should be the head of the
church. In 588 A.D. the patriarch of Constantinople,
John the Faster, assumed the title of "Universal Bishop
of the Church." This was bitterly contested by the
pope of Rome. In 606 A. D., the emperor took the title
of "Universal Bishop" away from John the Faster
and conferred it upon Boniface III then Pope of Rome.

11 *Matt.* 5:13-16.

Thus papal supremacy was formally introduced. The date, 606 A.D. really marks the beginning of what is now known as the Roman Catholic Church, in a fully organized state, with the pope of Rome as its head.

A study of these historical facts should impress us with the importance of keeping the church and civil government entirely separate. It is bad for both church and state, for either to seek to direct the affairs of the other.

QUESTIONS

1. Review.

2. What does the Bible teach as to the relation of the church and civil government?

3. To what extent does God require his children to submit to civil law?

4. Tell of Constantine's conversion.

5. How long did he postpone his baptism? Why?

6. What significance may be attached to this?

7. Relate some of the good results of Constantine's conversion to the church?

8. What were some of the good results to the state?

9. Mention and discuss some of the evil results.

10. What means does God will that the church use to influence the world?

11. In the events under consideration, which was more influenced by the other, the church or the world?

12. Make practical applications of this to the church in its relation to the world today.

13. What‾ is monasticism?

14. When and by whom was it founded?

15. Describe the conditions that gave rise to this movement.

16. How does this idea contradict the principles of Christianity?

17. The capital of the Roman Empire was moved from Rome to what city? When?

18. Having lost her place as capital of the Empire, what did Rome seek to be?

19. Describe the battle for power in which the five patriarchs engaged?

20. Whom did the emperor designate as the first "Universal Bishop?" When?

21. What marked the actual beginning of the Roman Catholic Church?

Chapter V.

THE CHURCH DURING THE DARK AGES
(Concluded)

In our last study we saw how the patriarch at Rome succeeded in gaining the preeminence over the patriarchs in four other cities. The power of the Pope of Rome was formally and legally recognized when, in 606 A. D., the emperor designated Boniface III as the "Universal Bishop of the Church." In this lesson we trace the development of the power of the Pope until he becomes the head of both the church and the state.

I. THE CULMINATION OF PAPAL POWER

The growth of papal power was gradual. The popes took the place of the Roman emperors as the rulers of Italy and later during the time of Charlemagne assumed the power of crowning the kings of Europe. As the power of the pope increased, it met with resistance on the part of many kings and princes. Bitter controversies occurred. One of the most notable of these took place between Henry IV of Germany and Pope Gregory VII, or Hildebrand. Among other acts of discipline which he directed toward Henry IV's reign, Pope Gregory excommunicated five of Henry's councellors who had been guilty of simony. Henry IV, feeling keenly the threat of his own power, called together the bishops of the Holy Roman Empire and compelled them to depose Gregory as pope. The pope then exercised his power and absolved all of Henry's subjects from allegiance to him. Since the pope had great power over the people, Henry was left without a kingdom. In order to be forgiven by the pope and reinstated as king, Henry was forced to lay aside his royal garments and make a journey over the Alps in the dead of winter and approach the pope in his palace at Canossa. After being forced to stand outside the castle for three days, with his bare feet in the snow, he was admitted into the pope's presence on bended knees.

"Another famous instance occurred later during the time of Pope Innocent III, who deposed John as King of England for opposing the Papal authority." [1]

Innocent III believed that he was the "Vicegerent of God upon earth."[2] He believed himself to be the successor to St. Peter and that he possessed "authority, not only over the church, but over the world."[3]

II. CATHOLIC CLAIM FOR THE POPE TODAY

At this point, we raise the question as to the power that is claimed by the pope of Rome today. Does the pope still consider himself the successor to St. Peter? Does he still believe that the authority to rule over the world in both religious and civil affairs rightfully belongs to him? Does the Catholic Church still believe that such power should be exercised by the pope, or have Catholics changed? The only fair way to answer

---

1 Frank Pack, *Lessons in Church History* (Chattanooga, 1940), 18.

2 John McClintock and James Strong, *Biblical, Theological and Ecclesiastical Cyclopedia,* eds., 12 vols. (New York, 1891), IV 591.

3 Fisher, *History Of The Christian Church,* 192.

this question is to allow Catholics to speak for themselves. Archbishop James Cardinal Gibbons states:

> The Church did not die with Peter. It was destined to continue till the end of time; consequently, whatever official prerogatives were conferred on Peter were not to cease at his death, but were to be handed down to his successors from generation to generation. The Church is in all ages as much in need of a Supreme Ruler as it was in the days of the Apostles. Nay, more; as the Church is now more widely diffused than it was then, and is ruled by the frailer men, it is more than ever in need of a central power to preserve its unity of faith and uniformity of discipline. Whatever privileges, therefore, were conferred on Peter which may be, considered essential to the government of the Church are inherited by the Bishops of Rome, as successors of the Prince of the Apostles; just as the Constitutional powers given to George Washington have devolved on the present incumbent of the Presidential chair. [4]

The January, 1946, issue of *The Converted Catholic Magazine* carried an article entitled "Pope Pius XII" which began as follows:

> The Prompta Bibliotheca, an official Roman Catholic almanac published by the press of Propaganda Fide in Rome, in its article under "Papa," states: "The Pope is of so great dignity and so exalted that he is not a mere man, but as it were, God, and the Vicar of Christ. The Pope is of such lofty dignity that, properly speaking, he has not been established in any rank of dignity, but has been placed upon the very summit of all ranks of dignities. He is likewise the Divine Monarch and Supreme Emperor, and King of Kings. The Pope is of so great authority and power that he can modify, explain or interpret even divine laws."

Regarding the power which the pope would like to exercise over the whole world through the Catholic Church, the same issue of *The Converted Catholic Magazine* continued:

> There is nothing incidental or accidental about the aims and activities of the Roman Catholic church. It uses expediency to gain its ultimate aims while biding its time

---

4 James Cardinal Gibbons, *Faith of Our Fathers,* 94th. Revised and Enlarged Edition (Baltimore), 108.

to entrench itself in a democratic country like the United States. Pope Leo XIII set forth this expedient policy in his instructions sent to the bishops of the United States in 1888: Although on account of the extraordinary political conditions today it may happen that the Church in certain modern countries acquiesces in certain modern liberties, not because she prefers them in themselves, but because she judges it expedient that they should be permitted, she would in happier times resume her own liberty.

As to Pope Leo's statement, *The Converted Catholic Magazine* offers the following comment:

The 'liberty' here intended is the traditional power of the Catholic Church to impose its dogmatic authority upon the entire world. Again in his encyclical Longinqua Oceani (Jan. 6, 1895), Pope Leo warned the bishops of America as follows: It is necessary to destroy the error of those who might believe, perhaps that the status of the Church in America is a desirable one, and also the error that in imitation of this sort of thing the separation of Church and State is legal and even convenient.

In view of the facts of history and of the official claims of the popes down through the years, it is timely that a warning be sounded. Such a note has been well expressed in the following quotation:

Our democracy was founded upon the idea of freedom of worship and a complete separation of church and state. These two institutions have entirely different spheres and the spheres of distinction are defined by the Constitution. Any tendency to bring church and state together must be viewed with alarm on the part of all lovers of freedom. This accounts for the protest of many Protestants who viewed with dismay the . . . move of this government to send an envoy to the Papal Court as a representative of this government. If the Catholic head is thus recognized when being only a figurehead as an earthly ruler, why not recognize every religious group in this country thus? 5

III. PETER WAS NOT A POPE

It is evident to the casual student that the whole foundation of Catholicism rests upon the pope and his

5 Pack, *Church History,* 18, 19.

authority. Remove the power of the pope and Catholicism crumbles. It is further evident to the casual student that the authority of the pope rests upon the one
proposiion as to whether Peter was a pope. Catholics
claim that Peter was the first pope and that the pope
of Rome today is the successor to Peter.

Refute the erroneous claim that Peter was the
first pope, and you have destroyed the authority of the
pope of Rome. With his authority gone, Catholicism
comes crashing down when viewed from a scriptural
standpoint.

Peter was not a pope because Christ, and not Peter,
is the basic foundation of the church. Jesus said to
Peter, "And I also say unto thee, that thou art Peter,
and upon this rock I will build my church; and the
gates of Hades shall not prevail against it." [6] To in-
terpret this statement of Jesus to mean that He would
build His church upon Peter is a mistake for two reasons: 1. It ignores the difference in the two words
rendered *Peter* and *rock*.

> The name 'Peter' here means "a stone" [7] and in the
> masculine gender . . . "Rock" here is feminine and refers
> to the foundation upon which Jesus built his church.
> "Petros" which means "a stone" is one thing, and "Petra"
> which means a "ledge of rock" is another. Jesus did not
> say nor mean to say that his church would be built upon
> a "a stone,' but upon a solid "ledge of rock." [8]

Peter had just confessed that Jesus was the Son of
God. Peter was to be as a stone in preaching the gospel
of Christ, but the church was to be built upon the bed-
rock foundation fact of the divinity of Christ. 2. To
say that Christ promised to build his church upon

6 *Matt.* 16:18.
7 *Jno.* 1:42.
8 H. Leo Boles, *A Commentary On The Gospel According To Matthew* (Nashville, 1936), 344, 345.

Peter is to contradict a plain passage of scripture. Paul said: "For other foundation can no man lay than that which is laid, which is Jesus Christ." [9] If Peter was the first pope, then he was the foundation upon which Christ built His church but, if Peter was the foundation of the church, then Paul was an imposter because he declared that Christ is the foundation and the only foundation upon which men can build their hopes. If Peter was the foundation of the church, to say that he must have successors is to say that a foundation succeeds a foundation under a building!

Peter was a married man, [10] but popes do not marry!

Those who recognize the authority of the pope dare not rebuke him for his conduct. It is evident that Paul did not regard Peter as pope because he rebuked him without any mention of his supremacy. [11]

Peter would not permit men to worship him, [12] but the pope of Rome expects men to bow down to him and he is addressed by his subjects as "Lord the Pope." Therefore Peter was not a pope.

IV STRANGE DOCTRINES

While this drastic change in the organization of the church was taking place, there gradually came into prominence a system of strange doctrines which fixed themselves in the religious practices of the day. Space will only permit brief mention of some of these false doctrines which were introduced between the second and the fourth centuries.

---

9. *1 Cor. 3:11.*
10 *Luke* 4:38.
11 *Gal.* 2:11-14.

12 *Acts* 10:25, 26.

1. Holy Water—said to be especially blessed and sanctified by the priest.

2. Penance—The infliction of punishment in expiation of sin and as evidence of one's penitence.

3. Latin Mass.

4. Images of Saints and Martyrs.

5. Extreme Unction—Annointing the body of those thought to be dying.

6. Purgatory.

7. Instrumental Music in the Worship—This is still not used by the Greek Catholics.

8. Transubstantiation. By prayer of pope or priest, the bread and wine of the Lord's Supper are said to be changed to the literal flesh and blood of Christ.

9. Celibacy—the popes and priests are forbidden to marry. This doctrine was prophesied in I Tim. 4:1-3.

10. Indulgences. "The doctrine of indulgences, or of the authoritative remission of penances by the substitution for them of prayers, benevolent gifts, or other forms of devotion and self-sacrifice, was universally accepted." [13]

11. Auricular Confession—Confessing one's sins into the ears of the priest that they may be forgiven.

12. Sprinkling for baptism.

Thus far, in this series of lessons, we have seen how far man will go into error when he cuts loose from the New Testament pattern for the church. The world today needs to learn that we must walk by God's word alone in religion or our worship and service becomes vain and useless. We should reject all doctrines that cannot be found in the Bible.

---

13 Fisher, *op. cit.,* 15.

QUESTIONS

1. Brief review of Lesson IV.

2. Whose place did the pope's take in the rule of Italy?

3. During the time of Charlemagne, what power did the pope assume in Europe?

4. How did many kings and princes react to this?

5. Tell of the controversy between Henry IV and Gregory VII.

6. What claim of authority was held by Innocent III?

7. Does this differ fundamentally from the claim that is made for the pope today by the Catholic Church? Give reasons for your answer.

8. Give scriptural arguments against the idea that Peter was pope.

9. Tell what you know of the twelve "Strange Doctrines" listed on page 48.

(The teacher should make special assignments in advance asking students to gather all information possible on these doctrines).

Chapter VI.

THE REFORMATION

In these lessons thus far, we have made a study of the Medieval Church, or the "Dark Ages." At the close of that period, Papal authority in religious matters was in full swing everywhere. Papal domination was sought and gained even in political affairs. In many instances, the Catholic Church resorted to carnal warfare in order to increase its power. The masses were in total ignorance of the Bible. It was truly the "Dark Ages." Simony, the custom of selling church offices to the highest bidder, was a universal practice. Miscellaneous money-making schemes, such as indulgencies and confessionals, were a source of rich profits to the church. "While the Papacy tightened its grip upon the Catholic Church, and set itself against all reform of any king, there arose some dissenting voices, who protested against the immorality among the clergy and spoke strongly against papal interference in political affairs." [1]

I. BEGINNINGS OF RELIGIOUS REFORM

Gleams of light began to shoot through the darkness as individuals made attempts to reform the Catholic Church. D'Aubigne calls these movements "Protestantism before the reformation." [2] Fisher speaks

---

1 Pack, *Church History*, 23.
2 J. H. Merle D'Aubigne, *History Of The Reformation Of The Sixteenth Century*, 5 vols., (New York, 1859), I, 88.

of them as "Reformers before the reformation." [3]   At this time we shall call attention to five of these early movements which arose for reform in the church. However, the world was not ready for them and they were repressed with bloody persecution.

1. The Albigenses became prominent in Southern France about 1170 A. D. They were opposed to traditions as authority in religion; they were opposed to the doctrines of purgatory and image-worship. They recognized the authority of the New Testament and circulated it to the extent of their ability.   They were extirpated in a great slaughter as the result of a call for a crusade against them by Pope Innocent III.

2. The Waldensians were founded by Peter Waldo about A. D. 1170. Waldo was a merchant of Lyons who appealed to the Scriptures in his opposition to the practices of the Roman Catholic Church. The Waldensians were noted for their zeal for purity of life. Under the fire of persecution, they left France and found hiding places in the valleys of Northern Italy.

3.   John Wycliffe (1324-1384) was an Englishman by birth; he was a graduate of Oxford University. History calls him "The Morning Star of the Reformation" because he was the first to distinguish himself in fighting against the Catholic Church along certain lines. Some of the things which he opposed were the authority of the Pope, the doctrine of Transubstantiation, and auricular confessions.

The greatest work of Wycliffe for the enlightenment of the world was the translation of the Bible into the English language. [4] "Excluded from Oxford in 1382 he retired to Lutterworth where he died. Years after his death his ene-

3 Fisher, History of *The Christian Church*, 271.
4 J. W. Shepherd, *The Church, The Falling Away, And The Restoration*, (Cincinnati, 1929), 75.

mies had his body dug from the grave and burned and his ashes scattered on a brook that flowed into Avon River. Wordsworth later celebrated this in his Ecclesiastical Sonnets by symbolizing the spread of his doctrine to all the world as the waters of the ocean washed all the shores with his ashes." [5]

4.   John Huss (1369-1415) was an outstanding reformer who lived in Bohemia. A Priest of the Catholic Church, he became a disciple of Wycliffe. With great zeal he exalted the Scriptures above tradition and human dogma and opposed the tyranny of the clergy. He fiercely denounced the sale of the indulgences. He was summoned to the Council of Constance and tried as a heretic. Although he had been promised safety by the emperor, he was burned to death in July, 1415.

5.   John Wessel (1420-1498) was a reformer of less renown than Wycliffe and Huss. However, he attacked Catholicism in some of its principal features. He avowed many of the same beliefs which were later taught by Luther. [6]

6.   Jerome Savonarola (1452-1498) lived in Florence, Italy. He denied the authority of the pope and made a bitter fight against the immorality of the clergy. Fisher states:

When the pope found that he could not bribe the powerful preacher with the offer of a cardinal's hat, nor reduce him to silence by repeated admonitions, he excommunicated him. Savonarola pronounced this excommunication void, as contradictory to the wise and just law of God. [7]

He was finally arrested. While in prison he wrote a tract on the fifty-first Psalm in which he set forth his ideas of justification. He was tried, condemned, and on May 23, 1498, he was burned to death in the square at Florence in front of the church where he had preached so long.

II. FORCES WHICH PREPARED THE WAY FOR THE REFORMATION.

As already pointed out, these early efforts at reform were soon repressed for they were somewhat premature in view of the governing circumstances. However, certain forces were in action during this period which were serving to prepare the way for a far-reaching movement which today is known as the Protestant Reformation or Revolution. Let us give brief notice to a number of these causes.

1. There was an awakening in Europe to a new interest in literature, art and science; the change from medieval to modern aims and methods of thought. The minds of the people had become darkened with superstition, ignorance and bigotry. This renewed interest in learning served to lift the veil of ignorance and superstition and inspired independence of thought. As the amount of information increased there was also an increase in dissatisfaction with the prevailing religious condition.

2 Another factor which paved the way for the Reformation was the invention of the printing press by Gutenberg in 1455. This made possible the printing of books from movable type. Soon books were being distributed by the thousands. Hurlbut states:

Before this invention, from the beginning of time, books had been circulated only as rapidly as they could be copied out by hand. A Bible in the Middle Ages cost the wages of a working man for a year. It is significant as showing the desire of that time, that the first book printed by Gutenberg

was the Bible. The press brought the Scriptures into common use, and led to their translation and circulation in all
languages of Europe. The people who read the New Testament soon realizd that the papal church was far from the
New Testament ideal. 8

In this historical fact we see a demonstration of
the power of God's word to enlighten the hearts of
men and expel the darkness of superstition, ignorance and tradition. As it was then, so has it ever
been and so it is today. The more people know of God
the greater will be their distaste for the traditions
and superstitions of men.

3.   There was a growing spirit of nationalism
which affected the thinking of the people and fed the
desire for greater freedom in religion.   Patriotism
caused many to resent the idea of submitting to for-
eign rule over their own national churches. They dis-
liked the idea of the pope, in another land, appointing
their church officers. Some refused to contribute
"Peter's Pence" for the support of the pope and the
erection of magnificent church buildings in Rome.

The seeds which produced the Reformation were
beginning to germinate. At the first the hand of persecution cut off each effort at reformation, but the idea
was spreading and finally it gathered such momentum
that it was able to march on in spite of efforts to crush
it.

III. THE REFORMATION PROPER— MARTIN LUTHER (1483-1546)

The only logical place to begin a study of what
might be called the "Reformation Movement Proper"
is with Martin Luther. He is known as "the hero of

8 Hurlbut, *Story Of The Christian Church,* 151.

the Reformation." Some said that "Luther, apart from the Reformation, would cease to be Luther." The son of a miner, he was born at Eisleben, Germany, November 10, 1483. He was reared under rigid discipline by parents who were poor, but self-respecting. The severe discipline of home and school, and the privations of early life prepared him for later hardships and trials. His early ambition was to study law. After reading a copy of the Bible for the first time, he changed his plans against his father's will. He entered a monastery at the age of twenty-one and studied in earnest. He later said "If ever a monk got to heaven by monkery, I would have gotten there." [9] He became a preacher at Wittenberg and also taught in the university in 1508.

Pope Leo X was eager to complete St. Peter's Cathedral in Rome. A number of papal agents were sent out to sell indulgences as a means of raising money. A man by the name of John Tetzel proved to be a super-salesman. Luther questioned the whole system of indulgences and vigorously opposed it. In October, 1517, he posted, on the church door at Wittenberg, ninety-five propositions, or theses, condemning the practice of indulgences and challenged anyone to debate with him. This, of course, caused a reaction, both favorable and unfavorable, all over Germany. Many souls rejoiced at the boldness of Luther. A great controversy followed. The dispute made Luther realize that human authority was against him and that it was necessary for him to plant his feet upon the Scriptures more distinctly.

9 Shepherd *The Church,* 93.

On June 15, 1520, Leo X issued a papal bull which gave Luther 60 days to change his course. On December 10, of that year, Luther burned the pope's decree at the city gate. By this act he threw off his allegiance to the Roman Church. During the year 1520 he had clearly expressed his views on vital issues. He published three pamphlets in which he opposed the sanctity of the priesthood. He called upon the nobles to throw off the bondage of Rome and take over the lands and wealth that was held by the Church. He challenged the authority of the pope and condemned the sacramental system, and he set forth his views on the subject of salvation. On January 3, Pope Leo issued a bull of excommunication. Four months later, the Diet of the Holy Roman Empire declared Luther an outlaw, but he found protection in the castle of Frederick, Elector of Saxony.

Luther was summoned to the Diet of Worms by the Emperor, Charles V, in 1521. At the trial, when the assembly called upon him to retract his statements, he said, "Unless I am persuaded by means of the passages which I have quoted, and unless they thus render my conscience bound by the word of God—I cannot and will not retract . . . Here I stand, I cannot do otherwise so help me God." On his way from Worms, he was seized by masked horsemen who took him to Wartburg Castle where he remained in safety for almost a year. He died at the age of sixty-three, February 18, 1546, while on a visit to his birthplace at Eisleben.

QUESTIONS

1. Describe the state of affairs at the close of the Medieval Period.

2. What caused the failure of the earliest attempts to reform the Catholic Church?

3. Who were the Albigenses?

4. Who were the Waldensians?

5. Tell of the work of John Wycliffe.

6. Who was John Huss?

7. Tell what you know about John Wessel.

8. Tell of the work and of the death of Jerome Savonarola.

9. Discuss the forces which prepared the way for the Reformation.

10. Why is Martin Luther's name so prominently connected with the Reformation?

11. When did he live?

12. Learn what you can of John Tetzel and be prepared to relate it in class.

13. What act of Luther's openly marked him as opposed to the corrupt practices of the Roman Church?

14. What was the Diet of Worms?

15. Quote the now famous words which Luther utered at the Diet of Worms.

Chapter VII.

THE REFORMATION (No. 2)

The church of our Lord was founded upon the first Pentecost after the resurrection of Christ. Its pattern is to be found in the New Testament. It was characterized by unity of doctrine, name, worship, and organization. True to warnings given by inspired writers, a great apostasy took place. The organization of the church was changed; a system of strange doctrines was introduced; and out of the ecclesiastical heirarchy which developed came the pope of Rome who was finally recognized as the head of both the church and the state. Voices that were raised against the power of the pope and the corrupt practices of the clergy were stilled by the hand of persecution. But, in the early part of the 16th century Martin Luther defied the authority of the pope and started a movement which was destined to shake the world, unchain the Bible from the pulpit and again place it in the hands of men and women who had long been hungering and thirsting after righteousness.

As we engage in a study of this kind, we may not only learn how and why so many denominations exist today, but we may also come to appreciate the sacrifices that were made by Luther and others who had the courage to stand for their convictions at any cost. As our hearts swell with gratitude for these great men, we must not overlook the fact that they were human and, therefore, were subject to making mistakes. We should accept what they taught only when it is the truth.

I. WILLIAM TYNDALE (1484-1536)

Another great reformer, whose work led the way to the overthrow of the power of Rome in England, was William Tyndale. He was born at Worcester about 1484. It became his chief desire in life to give the common people the Bible in their own language. He said to a religious teacher of his time, "If God spare my life, I will cause a boy that driveth the plough shall know more of the Scripture than thou dost."[1] He fulfilled this purpose.

The story of the sacrifices and persecutions which Tyndale suffered in order to translate the Bible into English is one of the most touching accounts in the lives of the reformers. Of course, Tyndale made many enemies. Some of them thirsted for his blood. In May, 1535, he was betrayed by a man who posed as his friend and invited him into his home to dine. Upon arriving at the home, his would-be host had him arrested. "On Friday, October 6, 1536, he was strangled at the stake and his body then burned to ashes. At the stake, with a fervent zeal and a loud voice, he cried: 'Lord, open the King of England's eyes.' "[2] Thus ended the life of William Tyndale, but his influence as an apostle of liberty lives on.

II. ULRICH ZWINGLI (1484-1564)

Ulrich Zwingli was a noted reformer who lived in Switzerland about the time of Martin Luther. He was born about 1484. He was slain on the battlefield by

1 Fisher, *History Of The Christian Church*, 346, 347.
2 Shepherd, *The Church*, 88.

Catholic soldiers while serving as a chaplain in the army which was defending Zurich, Switzerland. [3] The principal difference in the attitudes of Luther and Zwingli as reformers was that Luther wanted to retain in the church all that was not expressly contradicted in the scriptures, while Zwingli wanted to abolish all that could not be proved by scripture. Therefore, Zwingli's reformation was the more complete.

III. JOHN CALVIN (1509-1564)

John Calvin, who was born in France, entered Switzerland and became Zwingli's successor as a reformer. The principal doctrines set forth by Calvin were predestination, particular redemption, total hereditary depravity, effectual or irresistible grace, and perseverance of the saints. "Calvin's Doctrines were taken by John Knox to Scotland and resulted in the establishment of the Presbyterian Church in that country." [4]

IV. THE RISE OF DENOMINATIONALISM

As the great Reformation movement gained momentum it soon became evident that the work of each outstanding reformer would result in the beginning of a new religious group. The general spirit of the movement was not to restore the New Testament order of things but rather to reform the then existing system of religion by attempting to correct the undesirable features. Each reformer directed his efforts toward some particular error or errors and as his followers in-

---

3 Fisher, *History Of The Christian Church,* 310.
4 Pack, *Church History,* 27.

creased in number a formal statement of faith and practice was adopted and thus a new religious denomination was born.

Let us now consider a brief account of how and when the leading denominations came into being. This account is based upon such facts only as can be supported by reliable authorities in the field of church history. The author's only desire in presenting these facts is to impart information and help the interested public to have a clearer understanding as to why there are so many religious groups in existence today.

As all New Testaments students know, denominationalism was unknown in New Testament times. [5] The first few denominations were off-shoots from Catholicism. As time passed, many others appeared as "off-shoots" of the "off-shoots" until there seems to be no end to the number that may come into existence.

V. THE LUTHERAN CHURCH (1521)

The first prominent denomination to come into being after the Protestant Reformation was the Lutheran Church. It resulted from the work of Martin Luther in 1521. This group adopted the Augsburg Confession of Faith in 1530. The establishment of the Lutheran Church was a vast stride from Rome, but it was far short of Jerusalem. The people who became members of the Lutheran church merely experienced a change of religious masters; they freed themselves from the Pope, but bound themselves by a man-made creed.

Some of the chief doctrines of the Lutheran Church are as follows: 1. Justification by faith only.

_____

5 *1 Cor.* 1:10; *Jno.* 17:20, 21.

This doctrine contradicts the teaching of James and Paul. [6] 2. That the denominations are branches of Christ or of the church. This is refuted by Christ's statement in John 15:1,6. 3. That the ten Commandments are binding upon men today. But the Bible teaches that only such commandments are binding today as are incorporated in the teaching of Christ and his apostles. 4. That the mode of baptism is non-essential. But, the New Testament plainly teaches that baptism is a "burial." [7]   5. That baptism in the law of Christ takes the place of circumcision under the law of Moses. But, it cannot be established by the Bible that baptism takes the place of anything. It is a commandment of the gospel of Christ given as a condition of forgiveness of sins. An interesting fact about Luther's attitude is that he pleaded with his followers to leave his name alone and be content to call themselves "Christians."

VI. THE PRESBYTERIAN CHURCH (1560)

As has been stated, the Presbyterian Church was an outgrowth of Calvinism under the leadership of John Knox about 1560. Presbyterianism became the established religion of Scotland in 1592. "The name 'Presbyterian,' unlike 'Lutheran,' is not derived from any man's name, nor does it describe any set of doctrines. It is rather descriptive of the form of church government. It is the anglicizing of the Greek noun presbyteros, which means elder, therefore, signifies a church governed by elders, in the literal meaning of the term." [8]

---

6 *James* 2:21-26; *Rom.* 5:1.
7 *Rom.* 6:4.
8 *Pack*, Church History, 28.

Among the doctrines taught by Presbyterians are to be found 1. predestination; 2. direct operation of the Holy Spirit; 3. infant baptism; 4. and that it is not necessary to eat the Lord's Supper every Lord's day. All of these doctrines are out of harmony with New Testament precept and practice. "The creed now regarded as standard among nearly all Presbyterians is the Westminister Confession of Faith, formulated by the Westminister Assembly, which met in London in July 1643 and continued its sessions for six years, meeting for 1163 times." [9]

As late as May 1938 the Southern Presbyterians voted 151 to 130 to strike out two sections of their creed on predestination. Has the *truth* changed? If the Presbyterian Creed was right before 1938, why did they vote to change it? If it was wrong before 1938 what assurance can they have that it is not still wrong on many things? In the next lesson we shall give an account of the beginning of other prominent denominations. Already we can see that for men to impose uninspired creeds and confessions of faith upon others only results in division and confusion. We must never lose sight of the New Testament pattern for the church. We can know that we are meeting with divine approval in our religious endeavors only as we adhere to the teachings of Christ and his apostles.

QUESTIONS

1. What two great lessons may be learned from a study of this kind?

9 *Ibid.*

2. What should always be kept in mind while studying the life and work of any great man in church history?

3. Where was William Tyndale born? When?

4. What great contribution did he make toward the spiritual enlightenment of his people?

5. Tell of his death.

6. Of what country was Ulrich Zwingli a native?

7. How did he meet his death?

8. State the principal difference in the attitudes of Luther and Zwingli as reformers.

9. Are these two attitudes manifest in modern movements in religion? Give reasons for your answer.

10. In what country was John Calvin born?

11. He is thought of as successor to what reformer?

12. Be prepared to name and explain briefly the principal doctrines set forth by Calvin.

13. By whom were Calvin's doctrines taken into Scotland and with what result?

14. What was the result of the work of each outstanding reformer?

15. What was the first denomination to come into existence? When?

16. What creed was adopted by this group?

17. State the chief doctrines of this denomination and tell how the Scriptures refute them.

18. When and by whom was the Presbyterian Church founded?

19. What gave rise to its name?

20. Name some of the doctrines taught by this denomination.

21. History proves that what result is inevitable when men impose uninspired creeds and confessions of faith upon others?

Chapter VIII.

THE REFORMATION (No. 3)

Having traced the departures from the New Testament doctrine and organization of the church which culminated in the development of the papal system, we are now engaged in a study of the spread of denominationalism which resulted from the great movement to reform the Catholic Church. In Chapter VII it was pointed out that the work of Martin Luther culminated in the beginning of the Lutheran Church, and that the Presbyterian Church was founded by John Knox who preached the principal doctrines set in order by Calvin.

I. THE CHURCH OF ENGLAND OR EPISCOPAL CHURCH (1534)

The Church of England or Episcopal Church (1534) had its beginning when King Henry VIII severed the church from the rule of Rome about 1534. An entanglement of circumstances of both a religious and political nature led to England's break with Rome. It is unfair to both Henry VIII and the Church of England to leave the impression that the only cause for Henry's action was the desire to be granted a divorce. This played its part, but this was only what might be called the last link in a chain of events which led to the act of formally severing connection with Rome.

The seeds sown by Luther, Wycliffe, and Tyndale continued to bear fruit in England. Groups of honest individuals met secretly and read the New Testament.

The more informed they became in Holy Writ the more dissatisfied they became with the doings of Rome.

Henry VIII had made a series of severe attacks upon Martin Luther for which the Pope conferred upon him the title of "Defender of the Faith," a title which the King of England still wears. However, Henry VIII became involved in certain political issues which gave rise to antagonism with Rome. The question of Henry's divorce precipitated matters. Henry wished to secure a divorce from Catherine of Aragon who had been his faithful wife for twenty years. He wished to marry Anne Boleyn who was fresh from the courts of France. The Pope denied his petition for divorce, whereupon Henry separated the English church from the rule of the Pope. Parliament declared Henry the head of the Church of England. The church retained much of the ritual and form of Catholicism.

"It was planted in America by the colonists in Virginia and remained under the jurisdiction of the Bishop of London until the time of the Revolutionary War. Severing its connections with the mother church at the time when the United States became free, it has been known as the Protestant Episcopal Church in America. The creed of the church is expressed in the Thirty-Nine Articles of Faith and the Book of Common Prayer contains the rituals used in the services of the church. It takes its name from its form of church government, which is episcopal—rule by bishops, as opposed to presbyterian form of government—or rule by elders of the local congregation . . . within the American Church there are two groups, one known as the High Church and the other as the Low Church." [1]

The High Church is more like the Catholic in its form of worship than is the Low Church.

---

1 Pack, *Church History*, 29.

THE BAPTIST CHURCH (1608)

As the casual student readily observes, the name and nature of some of the denominations were determined by the form of church government adopted. However, in the early part of the sixteenth century a controversy arose which centered around the doctrine and practice of baptism and led to the founding of another religious group now known as the Baptist Church. Those who led in this controversy were given the name of Anabaptists, a term which means rebaptism. They were so-called because they refused to admit anyone into fellowship who would not repudiate his Catholic baptism by being baptized again.

From these later there grew up what we know today as Baptist Churches. There are some Baptist historians that have claimed they could trace a line of Baptist churches back through the centuries to the New Testament times by a chain of successive churches. However, the better informed scholars among them make no such claim. In fact, there is no religious group today that can trace itself back to New Testament times by a chain of successive churches. Catholics certainly cannot, since they have radically changed their worship and doctrines from the New Testament patterns. [2]

"The use of the term 'Baptist' as a denominational designation is of comparatively recent origin, first appearing about the year 1644." [3] "Baptist" is a "name first given in 1644 to certain congregations of English Separatists, who had recently restored the ancient practice of immersion." [4]

In the interest of fairness, the student should note what one outstanding Baptist scholar had to say

2 *Ibid*, 30.
3 *The New Schaff-Herzog Encyclopedia Of Religious Knowledge*, 13 Vols. (1908), I 456.
4 *The New International Encyclopedia*, 25 Vols., (Grand Rapids, 1927), II 646.

as to whether it is possible to trace the Baptist Church in unbroken succession to New Testament times.

> Little perception is required to discover the fallacy of a visible apostolical succession in the ministry (the Catholic claim), but visible church succession is precisely as fallacious, and for exactly the same reasons . . . The very attempt to trace an unbroken line of persons duly baptized upon their personal trust in Christ, or of ministers ordained by lineal descent from the apostles, or of churches organized upon these principles, and adhering to the New Testament in all things, is in itself an attempt to erect a bulwark of error.5

In giving an account of the work of John Smyth, who was the leader in formally organizing the Baptist Church, Armitage points out that Smyth "believed that the Apostolical Church model was lost, and determined on its recovery. He renounced the figment of a historical, apostolic succession, insisting that where two or three organize according to the teachings of the New Testament, they form as true a Church of Christ as that of Jerusalem, though they stand alone in the earth." 6

John Smyth was the leader of a group of separatists who fled from England to Holland to escape the persecutions of James I. They reached the conclusion that infant baptism was not taught in the Scriptures. Whereupon Mr. Smyth baptized himself and then baptized the others of the group. Many scholars maintain the belief that Smyth baptized himself by sprinkling. However, some recognized historians doubt this. Armitage states:

> With the design of restoring this pattern (the New Testament pattern), he (Smyth) baptized himself on his faith in Christ in 1608, then baptized Thomas Helwys with

5 Thomas Armitage, *A History Of The Baptist*, 2, 3.
6 *Ibid.*, 453.

about forty others, and so formed a new church in Amsterdam. In most things this body was Baptist, as that term is now used, with some difference. 7

With reference to Smyth's baptism, Armitage further states: "Whether he dipped himself is not clear, but all circumstances, with a few statements of that day imply that he did." 8

From these facts of history we must conclude that the Baptist church did not exist prior to the seventeenth century. That there were those before his time who believed in and practiced immersion for baptism, but that these composed the institution which is now known as the Baptist Church is a position which cannot be supported either by history or the Scriptures.

After the death of John Smyth, Thomas Helwys and a number of his brethren returned to England and founded the first Baptist Church there in 1611 under the name of General Baptists. Numerous divisions have occurred among the Baptists, and so today there are several groups of Baptists wearing differing denominational titles and with variations in doctrine on some points. While Baptists generally do not claim a formal creed or confession of faith, they do make use of church manuals which set forth the fundamental items of faith and rules of conduct in the work and worship of the church. Two of the most popular of these are, *The Standard Manual For Baptist Churches by* Edward T. Hiscox, published by the American Baptist Publication Society, and *Church Manual Designed For The Use Of Baptist Churches by* J. M. Pendleton, published by The Judson Press.

7 *Ibid.,* 454.   8 *Ibid.,* 457.

THE METHODIST CHURCH

As we now turn our attention to a brief history of the Methodist Church, the proper place to begin is with the life of John Wesley. He was born at Epworth, England in 1703. He was graduated from Christ Church College, Oxford, in 1724. He was ordained as a priest in the Church of England and was for a number of years a fellow of Lincoln College. In 1729 he became associated with a group of young men who were displeased with the lack of spirituality and the mere form and ritual which characterized the Church of England at that time. This group stressed holy living and were spoken of in derision as "the Holy Club." Fisher describes the activities of this group in the following language:

> One of their rules requires that they should frequently 'interrogate themselves whether they have been simple and recollected; whether they have prayed with fervor, Monday, Wednesday, Friday, and on Saturday noon; if they have used a collect at nine, twelve, and three o'clock; duly meditated on Sunday, from three to four, on Thomas A. Kempis (who wrote Imitation of Christ); mused on Wednesday and Friday, from twelve to one, on the passion. They frequently partook of the communion. They visited also alms houses and prisons, and were diligent in efforts to instruct and console the suffering. For the reason that they lived by rule, the term 'Methodist' was attached to them as a nickname by their fellow-students. [9]

Mr. Wesley and his associates did not intend from the first to start a new religious group, but desired only to reform the Church of England. The English church looked with disfavor upon their activities and finally a separate body took shape when the first Methodist Society was formed at Kingswood, near the city of Bristol, England, in 1739. Methodism was first

---

9 Fisher, *History of the Christian Church,* 515. For a striking portrayal of Methodism in the United States see *Life* Magazine, November 10, 1947.

planted in America in a formal way in 1766.

The Methodist Discipline is the creed of the church and also contains rules of action and church laws. The doctrines, laws, and rules of Methodism change from time to time. For this reason the Discipline is revised periodically. There had been so many changes in it by 1888 that Dr. P. A. Peterson could write a 247 page book entitled *The History Of The Revision Of The Discipline,* published by the Publishing House Of The Methodist Episcopal Church South, Nashville, Tennessee. Here is an example of the changes which are made in the Discipline: The edition of 1908 begins the ritual for baptism of infants with, "Dearly Beloved, forasmuch as all men are conceived and born in sin," while the edition of 1940 begins the same ritual with, "Dearly Beloved, forasmuch as all men are heirs of life eternal." In the edition of 1940 in an article entitled "Episcopal Address," it is stated: "We have, therefore, expected that the Discipline would be administered, not merely as a legal document, but as a revelation of the Holy Spirit working in and through our people." The article is signed by the president, vice president, and secretary of Bishops.

In view of this official claim by Methodists that their discipline is "a revelation of the Holy Spirit," it is in order to ask two questions: 1. If one believes the Discipline to be a revelation of the Holy Spirit, how can he also believe that the Bible is the complete and final revelation of God's will through the Spirit as it claims in 2 Tim. 3:16, 17? 2. If the Methodist Discipline is a revelation of the Holy Spirit, why is it necessary for man to keep changing it? Does the Holy Spirit change His mind from time to time?

Since the beginning of the Reformation movement, denominations have continued to multiply until they number in the hundreds. Time will not permit mention of them all. These facts have been presented in the hope of helping those interested in knowing why there are so many religious groups to a clearer understanding of these matters. It must be agreed that such a state of division would have never existed had all men held to the New Testament in its purity and simplicity down through the years.

QUESTIONS

1. Memorize the names together with the dates of beginning, of all the denominations mentioned in Chapters VII and VIII.

2. Relate the circumstances which led to the beginning of the Church of England.

3. By what name is this group known in the United States?

4. Who is recognized by historians as the founder of the Baptist Church?

5. Why were "Baptists" so called?

6. What mistaken idea do hundreds today (including many Baptists) have as to how Baptists derived this name?

7. What movement resulted in the beginning of the Methodist Church?

8. Whose name is most prominently connected with this movement?

9. How did this group come to be called "Methodists"?

10. What form of government is practiced by the Methodist Church? Explain.

1. What creed is used by this denomination?

12. Discuss some of the changes that have been made in it.

13. In view of these changes, what questions are in order?

14. How could denominationalism have been avoided?

Chapter IX

THE RESTORATION MOVEMENT

In our study of the Reformation it was found that the chief effort of this movement was to *reform* the Catholic Church. We now begin the study of another period in the history of the church by observing some facts about a great movement which had its beginning in the latter part of the eighteenth century in this country. It is known as the Restoration. As suggested by the title which has been given to this movement, the chief effort was to *restore* the New Testament pattern in worshipping and serving God.

CAUSES OF THE RESTORATION MOVEMENT

A number of causes combined to bring about this movement:

1. Since the beginning of the Reformation, the Bible had made great gains in circulation year by year. This increase in the circulation of the scriptures, of course, led to increased knowledge of the word of God. As men learned more of the word of God they thought less of human creeds. In the hearts of many the ques-

---

1 Materials taken from: Robert Richardson *Memoirs Of Alexander Campbell,* 2 vols. (Cincinnati, 1897); Homer Hailey, *Attitudes And Consequences* (Los Angeles, 1945); M. M. Davis, *How The Disciples Began And Grew* (Cincinnati, 1915); Shepherd, *The Church, The Falling Away, And The Restoration;* Leslie G. Thomas, *Restoration Handbook* (Nashville 1941; Pack, *Lessons In Church History.*

tion rang, "Why not go back to the Bible and do away with creeds"?

2. As the number of denominations continued to multiply and new creed books and confessions of faith were constantly being written and adopted, it became more evident that the Reformation Movement was failing to restore New Testament Christianity in its purity and simplicity.

3. The more men studied the New Testament the more they recognized the sin of religious division. They saw that denominationalism was preventing the answer to Christ's prayer for unity among his followers. They saw religious division was contrary to the pleadings of the apostle Paul. (1 Cor. 1:10; Eph. 4:4.) They saw that divisions were weakening the forces of God on every hand. They came to realize that each creed was an iron bed and the preacher was made to fit it.

4. Another condition which caused many honest seekers after the truth to get their eyes open to the need for restoring the ancient order of things was the ignorance and arrogance of the clergy. As in other fields of endeavor, so it is in religion—the more ignorant one is, the more arrogant he is apt to become. So, the clergy of the day was cursed with men who in their ignorance stood upon the stilts of arrogance and expected the world to look up to them. They assumed the right of legislation for those in the pews. Instead of leading their followers back to the New Testament, they stood in the way of reformation and restoration.

5. The Calvinistic doctrine of hereditary total depravity played its part in paving the way for the great movement to restore New Testament teaching.

The idea that all men are born totally depraved and that if a baby died it would be punished in an eternal hell was repulsive to logical minds. Some reacted by losing all interest in religion; others became infidels; while such a doctrine caused many to be filled with a greater desire for Bible doctrine.

THE PRINCIPLES OF THE RESTORATION MOVEMENT

The principles of the Restoration Movement may be summarized as follows:

1. Recognition of Christ as supreme authority in religion and the New Testament as the only rule of faith and practice. This would automatically do away with creeds and human authority.

2. A proper distinction between the Old and New Testaments.

3. Recognition of the New Testament pattern of the church.

4. The autonomy of the local church.

5. The unity of all Christians.

SOME LEADERS IN THIS MOVEMENT

Let it be clearly understood by all that Alexander Campbell was not the originator of this movement. Historical facts confirm this statement. The following men preceded the Campbells and did much to advance the cause of simple New Testament Christianity.

James O'Kelly (1794), a Methodist preacher in Mankintown, North Carolina, began to oppose the episcopal form of government in the Methodist Church. He insisted upon the autonomy of the local church as is found in the New Testament.

He and those who agreed with him withdrew from the Methodist Church and at a meeting in Surrey County, Virginia in 1794, the following points were emphasized: 1. Use the name "Christian" and no other. 2. Christ as the only head of the church: 3. The Bible as the only creed. 4. The right of private judgement and liberty of conscience.

Dr. Abner Jones (1800), a prominent Baptist preacher of Vermont, became distressed over sectarianism and, desiring to see it cease, broke away from the Baptists about 1800. He led in establishing congregations that endeavored to worship after the New Testament order, wearing the name "Christian" and accepting the Bible only as their rule of faith and practice. Dr. Jones had not heard of O'Kelly and his work, but he had his New Testament and he was seeking to get back to it.

Barton W. Stone (1801), was a bewildered young man who wanted to be saved but had failed to undergo any "experience" which, as he had been taught, was to be regarded as proof that he was one of the "elect." He was urged to preach by friends in the Presbyterian Church although he had received no "call" to preach and did not accept the Westminister Confession of Faith in full. He was assigned to preach at the Concord and Cane Ridge Churches in Kentucky in 1798. He preached that God loved all men and that Jesus died for all. He preached the Great Commission of Christ as it is revealed in the New Testament. In 1803, he attended the trial of Richard McNemar who was brought before the Presbytery of Ohio for preaching contrary to the Confession of Faith. He and five other preachers present knew they were guilty of the same offence so they withdrew from the Presbyterian Church and formed the "Springfield Presbytery." However, it was destined to be short-lived, for a year after it was formed they concluded that it was unnecessary and unscriptural. On June 28, 1804, they drew up and published an unique religious document entitled "The Last Will and Testament of Springfield Presbytery." [2] The following statements are contained in this document:

"1. We will that this body die, be dissolved, and sink into union with the body of Christ at large; for there is but one body and one Spirit, even as we are called in one hope of our calling.

"2. We will that our name of distinction, with its reverend title, be forgotten, that there be but one Lord over God's heritage and His name one.

"3.   We will that our power of making laws for the government of the church, and executing them by delegated authority, forever cease; that the people may have free course to the Bible, and adopt the law of the spirit of life in Christ Jesus.

"4.   We will that each particular church as a body, actuated by the same spirit, choose her own preacher, and support him by a freewill offering, with out a written call or subscription, admit members, remove offences; and never henceforth delegate her right of government to any man or set of men whatever.

"5.   We will that people henceforth take the Bible as the only sure guide to heaven; and as many as are offended with other books which stand in com-

---

2 F. L. Rowe, *Pioneer Sermons And Addresses*, Third Edition (Cincinnati, 1925), 7-10.

petition with it, may cast them into the fire if they choose, for it is better to enter into life having one book, than having many to be cast into hell."

What is there in these statements to which anyone could object who believes the Bible to be the compelte and final revelation of the will of God?

The work of these men, James O'Kelly, Dr. Abner Jones, and Barton W. Stone, in pleading for a return to the New Testament order of things was done each without the knowledge of what the others were doing. All of these men began their efforts in this direction a number of years before Alexander Campbell came to America. Before discussing Alxander Campbell it is in order that we give attention to the work of his father.

Thomas Campbell was born in County Down, Ireland, February 1, 1763, and died at Bethany, Virginia, in January, 1854. He was highly educated both for the ministry and for school work. He is described by those who knew him as a man of culture and learning; having a strong mind and a kind heart. He loved peace and hated religious division. He was filled with deep reverence for the word of God. He possessed the courage to stand for his convictions. He came to America because of ill health, arriving in this country May 27, 1807.

He was received by the Philadelphia Synod of the Presbyterian Church and was assigned to work in Washington County, Pennsylvania. Contrary to the rules of the church, he communed with members of other divisions of the Presbyterian Church. For this he was censured by the Presbytery. "He appealed to the Synod of North America, the highest governing body in his communion, but his position was not sustained." "Being persecuted, he withdrew from the Presbyterian Church and preached as an independent." He and a number of friends who stood for the same principles met at the home of Abraham Altars. In a speech upon that occasion, Mr. Campbell declared: "Where the Scriptures speak, we speak; where the Scriptures are silent, we are silent." On August 17, 1809, he and his followers formed the "Christian Association of Washington" and proceeded to draw up a statement of purpose which they called "Declaration, and Address." [3] This famous document contains more than 30,000 words.

The principal points of the "Declaration and Address" may be summarized as follows: 1. *The Unity of the Church.* "That the church of Christ on earth is essentially, intentionally, constitutionally one." 2. *Christian Fellowship.* That, although there must be separate local congregations, yet they should be one with no schisms and discord. 3. *Terms of Communion.* That nothing be required of Christians as articles of faith but what is expressly taught and enjoined upon them in the word of God. 4. *"That the New Testament is supreme authority for Christians in all matters of faith and practice."*

When Thomas Campbell and his associates renounced their allegiance to a creed and announced their purpose to be guided by the New Testament alone, they were unaware of what had been done by others already referred to, but they were taking steps in the same direction. Until this time, the renowned Alexan-

---

3 *Ibid.,* 14-104.

der Campbell was still a school-boy in Scotland. His work will be covered briefly in Chapter X. We shall investigate historical facts to learn whether Alexander Campbell was the founder of a denomination.

QUESTIONS.

1. What was the chief difference in the aims of the Reformation and the Restoration?

2. Discuss the causes of the Restoration Movement.

3. State the principles of the movement.

4. Tell what you know of the following: James O'Kelley; Dr. Abner Jones; Barton W. Stone.

5. What is "The Last Will And Testament Of Springfield Presbytery?" By whom was it drafted? When? For what purpose?

6. Discuss its principal points.

7. What Bible truths are contradicted in this document?

8. How long after the work of Alexander Campbell did O'Kelly, Jones, and Stone do their work?

9. Who was the father of Alexander Campbell?

10. Give a brief account of his life and work.

11. Tell about the "Declaration And Address," giving its principal points.

12. Did this work of restoring the New Testament order of things begin as an organized movement

or did individuals in widely separated areas launch independent efforts?

13.   What did all who were interested in this movement hold in common?

14.   Where was Alexander Campbell when this great movement had its beginning?

15.   Was he instrumental in beginning these initial efforts?

Chapter X.

THE RESTORATION MOVEMENT [1]

The latter part of the Eighteenth Century saw the
beginning of a great movement to restore the New
Testament pattern of the church upon the earth. This
movement had its beginning when preachers of various
denominations and in different parts of this country
recognized the sinful division existing among those
who claimed to follow Christ and sought to unite all
professed believers by renouncing denominational
creeds and pleading for the New Testament as the
only guide of faith and practice. In our study thus far
we have found the names of James O'Kelly, Abner
Jones, Barton Stone and Thomas Campbell prominently connected with this movement. Keep in mind
that these men started their work while Alexander
Campbell was still a young man in s c h o o l
in Scotland. He was not, therefore, the originator of
the movement.

After more than two years in this country,
Thomas Campbell was joined by his family September
29, 1809. The family, during this time, had been in the
charge of his son, Alexander.

Alexander Campbell, was born near Shane's Castle,
County Antrim, Ireland, September 12, 1788. He died
in Bethany, Virginia, now West Virginia, March 4,

---

1. Materials taken from same sources as Chapter IX.   See
footnote, page 75.

1866. Before coming to this country, Alexander Campbell attended the University of Glasgow, Scotland, and was greatly influenced by the Haldane brothers who preached Christian unity. Soon after his arrival in America he and his father spent much time in discussing religious subjects. His father showed him the proof sheets of the "Declaration And Address" to which reference has already been made. They were overjoyed to find that they had been giving thought to the same issues and that there was agreement between them.

Mr. Campbell and his father were troubled as they could see that the "Christian Association of Washington" was gradually taking shape as another denomination, a thing which was never intended. They were invited to join the Pittsburgh Synod. Mr. Campbell opposed it privately, but gave way to his father's judgment. On October 4, 1810, Thomas Campbell made application specifying that they were not to be Presbyterians, nor would they be governed by the laws of the Synod, but would only cooperate with them in their work. The application was rejected. On May 4, 1811, they formed an independent congregation which they called "Brush Run." It started with a membership of thirty. Most of these had been sprinkled in infancy. Some of them changed their convictions about baptism and requested immersion. However, the Campbell's were not convinced that infant baptism was unscriptural until the birth of Alexander's first child brought them face to face with the question. Being a thorough Greek scholar, Mr. Campbell went into the original with his investigations. He was soon convinced that a *penitent believer* was the only Bible subject for baptism. He was also convinced that the original word for *baptize* meant *immersion*. On June 12, 1812, Alexander Campbell and his father, together with other members of the family, were immersed in Buffalo Creek by Matthias Luce of the Baptist Church. However, it was thoroughly understood and agreed by Mr. Luce and those who were to be baptized that they were not to be required to give a "religious experience" as was practiced by the Baptists and that the only confession they were to make was the one made by Peter at Caesarea Philippi, that Jesus is "the Christ, the Son of the Living God." [2]

The stand which they now took on immersion made for them enemies among the Presbyterians and friends among the Baptists. Upon being urged to do so, they cast their lot with the Redstone Baptist Association in 1813 on the condition that they be "allowed to teach and preach what they learned from the Holy Scriptures." They withdrew from this association in 1816. In 1823 they joined the Mahoning Baptist Association. Later they severed all connection with the Baptists.

Lessons In Church History, by Frank Pack contains a brief summary of Mr. Campbell's work:

Alexander Campbell rapidly became the leading champion of the Restoration, advocating the principles his father set forth in the paper, the "Christian Baptist." He became one of the foremost Bible scholars of his day and also distinguished himself as a great debater. Always desiring the truth, he held several discussions with leading religious advocates. His chief debates were: the debate with Robert Owen on the Evidences of Christianity; the debate with Bishop John G. Purcell on Roman Catholicism; and the discussion with N. L. Rice on the Design of Baptism, infant Baptism and the work of the Holy Spirit . . . Alexan-

---

2 *Matt.* 16:17, 18.

der Campbell was interested in Christian education and founded Bethany College in order to train the young in the ways of Christian thinking and living. He kept the issues of his religious journal before the people to provoke thought and have a better understanding of the Restoration and its ideals brought to their attention. He did not formulate any creed, nor did he erect any organization. His whole desire was to find out what New Testament Christianity was and to try to bring about the same thing in his day. His life was filled with much useful service and preaching in the interest of undenominational Christianity.

Despite the great work done by the Campbell's, O'Kelly, Jones, Stone and others of their day, they were uninspired human beings and were therefore subject to mistakes as are all men. It would be a mistake to seek to defend any of them in all that they did or taught. They were right only in so far as they held to the teaching of the New Testament. When churches of Christ today preach the same things that were advocated by these men, it is not because *they* taught it, but because it is found in *the word of God*.

THE AMERICAN CHRISTIAN MISSIONARY SOCIETY

As time went by those in the various sections of the land who were pleading for a return to the New Testament became acquainted with one another and gradually united their efforts. But this great stride toward unity among Christ's followers was soon hindered by new movements which occurred within the ranks of those who had so recently sought to overcome the sin of denominationalism. From the time that connection had been severed with denominations and their associations the only church organization had by these simple Christians was that of the local church, such as may be found in the New Testament pattern.

In October, 1849, a convention was held in Cincinnati, Ohio, by some who desired a "general church organization for the furtherance of the work by the church collectively." At this convention the "American Christian Missionary Society" was organized. This, of course, met with bitter opposition from those who believed the church of the Lord to be the only institution by God for spreading the gospel of Christ. Thus the peace that had prevailed was threatened.

INSTRUMENTAL MUSIC

About ten years later another event occurred which proved to be the wedge that divided this great group of disciples who had been pleading for unity.

In 1858 or 1859, Dr. L. L. Pinkerton, who for a number of years "had served the church in Midway, Kentucky, as its minister," "introduced a melodeon into the congregation at that place." The question of instrumental music in the worship spread among the congregations causing division in many of them. Two separate groups were formed among these reformers ---the one contending for New Testament authority in all things; the other admitting the use of instruments of music and the organization of missionary societies on the ground that these are not forbidden in the New Testament. Through the years the liberal group, now known in the South as the Christian Church, or the Disciples' Church has continued to drift from the New Testament pattern until it can no longer truthfully claim to hold to the slogan that was coined in the early days of the Restoration, "Where the Bible speaks, we speak; where the Bible is silent, we are silent."

Many labor under the mistaken impression that the

only difference today in the churches of Christ and the Christian Church is that of instrumental music. But, this and the many other innovations which have been introduced by the Christian Church are only the results of a difference in attitude toward the Bible which holds these two bodies apart. This difference in attitude is recognized by Dr. A. W. Fortune, who has served as professor in the College of the Bible, Lexington, Kentucky, and has preached for the Central Christian Church of that city. In his book, *The Disciples in Kentucky,* page 383, Dr. Fortune states:

> The controversies through which the Disciples have passed from the beginning to the present time have been the result of two different interpretations of their mission. There have been those who believed it is the spirit of the New Testament church that should be restored, and in our method of working the church must adapt itself to changing conditions. There have been those who regarded the New Testament church as a fixed pattern for all time, and our business is to hold rigidly to that pattern regardless of the consequences. Because of these two attitudes, conflicts were inevitable.

While the Christian Church consists of two wings, one more conservative than the other, it is true that among Christian Churches the following may be found which churches of Christ do not practice or endorse: Missionary Societies; mechanical instruments of music; observance of the Lord's supper on Thursday evening in recognition of "Holy Week;" women preachers; women elders; the practice of selling merchandise, serving dinners, etc., to raise money for the church; pageants, cantatas, and other programs for entertainment; the dedication of babies; receiving the pious unimmersed into the fellowship of the church, and other things which could be mentioned.

The course that has been followed by the Christian Church of adopting virtually every new practice in religion that presents itself is a forceful demonstration of what will happen when men abandon the word of God as the all-sufficient guide in worshipping and serving Him.

A WORD OF WARNING

As has ever been true in the history of the church, it is true today that "the purity of the church, unity among brethren, and ultimate victory over the world" rests upon the attitude of the members toward the word of God and the pattern of the church revealed therein. The author is one of those who believes that the New Testament reveals a fixed pattern for the church of all time and that loyalty to Christ demands that we hold to that pattern. The church must not adapt itself to the changing conditions of the times if it means a departure from the divine pattern.

The cry that the church is not doing its duty along some lines is no justification for man-made schemes for doing the work of the church. The church of the Lord was in existence for more than sixty years before the New Testament was completed. It operated in all phases of its mission on full scale. This can be done today. Those who detect failure on the part of the church in any phase of its work should not attempt to "reform" conditions as they are, but they should set about to *restore* the pristine purity of the church in practice as well as doctrine.

In all of our thoughts of united effort and congregational cooperation, let us keep the church of the Lord free from institutionalism. Let it be overshadow-

ed by nothing; let nothing be tied to it, nor suffer it to
be tied to man-made organizations of any kind for
any purpose. In short, let us keep our eyes on the New
Testament pattern.

THE NEED TODAY

The author wishes to close this series of studies
in Church History with an appeal to all who read it
to remember that the Bible is the only authority needed in religion. The word of God is unchangeable.[3] Much
is being heard in this age about the need for a new
religion. Religious leaders are known to encourage
this notion. The plea is made that a new age needs a
new religion. A new religion for a new age? Who said
so? Not the man who believes that the word of God
shall stand forever. But such is the foolish babbling
of a blatant infidel! A new religion for a new age?
How could it be? When God made the sun, the air,
and the water, he made them to meet the physical
needs of his creature man. Man's physical needs are
the same today as they were in the beginning. When
God made Christianity, he made it to meet the spiritual
needs of his creature man. Man's spiritual needs are
the same today as they were two thousand years ago
when Christianity was born in the cradle of Palestine.
To talk of needing a new religion is as senseless as to
talk of needing a new sun to shine upon us, or a new
air to fill our lungs, or a new kind of water to slake
our thirst! A new religion for a new age? No! A
thousand times, No! What this old world needs is not
a new religion to meet the whims and notions of a
new generation. But, what it needs is to hear the old
time religion, the gospel of Christ, as it issues fresh

3 *Matt.* 24:32; *1 Pet.* 1:23.

from the breath of God through the pages of His eternal truth. This world needs to have the Bible and the Bible alone preached until the new generation forsakes its many unstable ideas that are born of fleshly lusts and worldly wisdom and falls upon its knees in humble recognition of the supreme authority of the word of God. Let us learn from the New Testament church the great lesson of depending upon the gospel of Christ alone as the power of God unto salvation.

QUESTIONS

1. Give a summary of Chapter IX.

2. When did Thomas Campbell's family join him in this country?

3. What university had Alexander Campbell attended before coming to America?

4. By what men had he been influenced and what did they preach?

5. What did discussions of religious subjects between Alexander Campbell and his father reveal?

6. Tell of events which led to the founding of "Brush Run" congregation.

7. What event quickened Mr. Campbell's interest in the subject of baptism and prompted a thorough investigation?

8. What were the results?

9. How did Presbyterians and Baptists react to the stand the Campbell's now took on immersion?

10. Tell of their connection with two Baptist associations.

11. Were they ever members of the Baptist Church?

12. Give a summary of Alexander Campbell's work as author, educator, evangelist and debater.

13. To what extent were these leaders of the Restoration right in their teaching and practices?

14. What condition arose within the ranks of those who were pleading for unity which hindered their efforts?

15. Tell of the beginning of the "American Christian Missionary Society."

16. Tell of the introduction of the mechanical instruments of music in the worship.

17. Name other innovations introduced and adopted by those who departed from the New Testament plan.

18. Discuss the difference in the attitude toward the Bible which drove the wedge that divided this great brotherhood.

19. What does the course followed by the Christian Church demonstrate?

20. Upon what do the purity of the church and unity among brethren depend?

21. Should the church depart from the divine pattern in order to adapt itself to the changing conditions of the times?

22. Instead of justifying the substitution of man-made schemes for the divine pattern by calling attention to the failure of the church in doing its duty, what should those who detect such failures attempt to do?

23. What is the need today in religion?

INDEX

Note: Material inside parentheses in quotations on pages 28, 29, 69, and 71 was supplied by the author to help in making clear the meaning of the quotations.